Especially for

Kenneth Cantley

From

Blair, Teresa, Danielle & Connor

Date

Dec. 25 - 2010

Sharing Christmas Every Day

A Keepsake Devotional
Featuring the Inspirational Verse of

Helen Steiner Rice

BARBOUR
PUBLISHING

A HELEN STEINER RICE ® Product

Published under license from the Helen Steiner Rice Foundation Fund, LLC.

ISBN 978-1-60260-860-3

Devotional writing provided by Patricia Mitchell in association with Snapdragon Group℠, Tulsa, OK.

Cover and interior illustration: Todd Williams

Published by Barbour Publishing, Inc., P.O. Box 719, Uhrichsville, Ohio 44683, www.barbourbooks.com

Our mission is to publish and distribute inspirational products offering exceptional value and biblical encouragement to the masses.

 Member of the
Evangelical Christian
Publishers Association

Printed in China.

Contents

Introduction

*W*e call it the most wonderful time of the year. Children make their wish lists months in advance, and by mid-November shoppers are flooding the stores. Christmas music and television specials dominate the airwaves, and trees with their festive decorations go up all over town. The weeks before Christmas are consumed with baking, wrapping packages, and addressing cards to friends and family. There are programs and cantatas, parties and fun going on everywhere we look. Yes, it's all quite amazing.

Even more amazing is that all these grand activities and preparations culminate in one small twenty-four-hour period. Sometimes, people get what they want out of that day; and more often, they don't.

How much better would it be to share the spirit of Christmas, the meaning of Christmas, the glory of Christmas every day, away from all the hype and commercialism surrounding that one little day in December? That's the question hidden in Helen Steiner Rice's beautiful poetry and the devotionals that follow. Couldn't we show love to our families, appreciate our friends, be kind to strangers, and revel in the gift of Christ all year long? Imagine what a wonderful year that would be!

THE BLESSING OF SHARING

Only what we give away
Enriches us from day to day,
For not in getting but in giving
Is found the lasting joy of living,
For no one ever had a part
In sharing treasures of the heart
Who did not feel the impact of
The magic mystery of God's love.
Love alone can make us kind
And give us joy and peace of mind,
So live with joy unselfishly
And you'll be blessed abundantly.

~HSR

SHARING WITH FAMILY

The Gift of a Lasting Love

Love is much more than a tender caress
And more than bright hours of happiness,
For a lasting love is made up of sharing
Both hours that are joyous and also despairing.
It's made up of patience and deep understanding
And never of stubborn or selfish demanding.
It's made up of climbing the steep hills together
And facing with courage life's stormiest weather.
And nothing on earth or in heaven can part
A love that has grown to be part of the heart.
And just like the sun and the stars and the sea,
This love will go on through eternity,
For true love lives on when earthly things die,
For it's part of the spirit that soars to the sky.

~HSR

LOVE UNCHANGING

Jesus Christ is the same yesterday and today and forever.
HEBREWS 13:8 ESV

*E*very family carries certain Christmas traditions from year
to year and generation to generation. Some go to church on
Christmas Eve, while others get up with their kids before dawn
on Christmas morning. Maybe Grandmother always stuffs the
turkey with oyster dressing or a certain aunt brings her amazing
cherry pie. Traditions like these bring families together and give
them a sense of heritage.

No matter how many traditions remain the same, however, no
Christmas is exactly like the last. Maybe there's the happy addi-
tion of a new in-law or grandchild, or the silent sorrow of a loved
one not present. Perhaps Christmas will be celebrated in a new
home, or under circumstances very different from last year's.

Time may have changed how you will celebrate Christmas
this year, but one thing time can never change—that's Jesus,
God's greatest gift to us. Through Jesus' birth, God showed His
compassion, His understanding, and His desire to embrace all
people. God and His love will never change, because God never
changes.

This Christmas, give thanks for the traditions you observe
from year to year, for new experiences and new traditions you
might begin, and most of all, for the people with whom you will
share this dearest of holidays.

WHAT IS LOVE?

What is love? No words can define it—
It's something so great only God could design it.
Wonder of wonders, beyond man's conception—
And only in God can love find true perfection. . . .
For love means much more than small words can express,
For what man calls love is so very much less
Than the beauty and depth and the true richness of
God's gift to mankind—His compassionate love. . . .
For love has become a word that's misused,
Perverted, distorted, and often abused.
To speak of light romance or some affinity for
A passing attraction that is seldom much more
Than a mere interlude of inflamed fascination,
A romantic fling of no lasting duration. . . .
But love is enduring and patient and kind—
It judges all things with the heart, not with the mind. . . .
And love can transform the most commonplace
Into beauty and splendor and sweetness and grace. . . .
For love is unselfish, giving more than it takes—
And no matter what happens, love never forsakes.
It's faithful and trusting and always believing,
Guileless and honest and never deceiving.
Yes, love is beyond what man can define,
For love is immortal and God's gift is divine!

~HSR

The Meaning of Christmas

"God so loved the world that He gave His only begotten Son, that whoever believes in Him should not perish but have everlasting life."

John 3:16

*B*oth the word *love* and the word *Christmas* mean different things to different people. For some, love is little more than a feeling of excited attraction, and Christmas is just a time to decorate and buy gifts. But for God's people, both words mean so much more!

For Christians, love is more than a feeling. It's a decision to give ourselves for others just as Jesus gave Himself for us. It speaks of sacrifice and unfettered kindness. Christmas celebrates the demonstration of that pure and unencumbered love. What could be more beautiful, more inspiring?

In response to the standard God Himself has set, we are also to give with purity of heart and show love in our actions as well as our words. What a wonderful opportunity we have at Christmas to reach out and share His great love with others.

The two words *Christmas* and *love* cannot be separated. As the holidays approach, reflect on the real meaning of Christmas and the love that inspired the first Christmas. As your heart fills with gratitude and joy, you will truly experience the reason for the season. Each gift, each ornament placed on the tree, each event, each preparation you make will shine forth more brightly than you ever thought possible.

THOUGHTS OF THANKS

At this time may God grant you
Special gifts of joy and cheer,
And bless you for the good you do
For others through the year....
May you find rich satisfaction
In your daily work and prayer,
And in knowing as you serve Him
He will keep you in His care.

~HSR

CARING HEARTS

The Spirit of the LORD will rest on him—
the Spirit of wisdom and of understanding,
the Spirit of counsel and of power,
the Spirit of knowledge and of the fear of the Lord.

ISAIAH 11:2 NIV

*I*n the circle of your family, who is it who always seems to know the right thing to say, the right thing to do, in all circumstances? This is the kind of person who doesn't hesitate to ask, "How can I help?" This is the kind of person you can depend on to be there when you need someone with a caring heart.

When Jesus was born on that first Christmas morning, God came into the world to make Himself that kind of person for you. No matter where you are in life right now, Jesus is there to celebrate with you, comfort you, strengthen you, and give you peace. His heart is filled with love for you, and He cares about your struggles and joys, your hardships and hopes. In His kindness, He provides help through the hands of your loved ones and gives your life purpose and meaning as you share your time and talents with others.

This Christmas, make it a point to show your appreciation for those in your family who are always there for you, and extend to them those small, daily courtesies that make even difficult circumstances sweeter and more pleasant. Most of all, give thanks to God, the giver of all, for the blessing of hearts that care.

A Special Prayer for You

I said a special prayer for you—I asked the Lord above
To keep you safely in His care and enfold you in His love.
I did not ask for fortune, for riches or for fame,
I only asked for blessings in the Holy Savior's name—
Blessings to surround you in times of trial and stress,
And inner joy to fill your heart with peace and happiness.

-HSR

A Powerful Gift

*This is my prayer: that your love may abound more and more
in knowledge and depth of insight.*

Philippians 1:9 niv

"I'm keeping you in my prayers." No doubt you have
heard people say this, and you probably have said it
yourself many times. Yet the commonly spoken phrase is
too often little more than a vague wish for better days or
a polite reply with no particular power behind it.

True prayer calls for passion and purpose, for action
and effort, and for time spent fully focused on God as you
bring the concerns of another person before His throne.
Your heavenly Father wants to hear you speak the desires
of your heart, and He is pleased to listen as you come to
Him on behalf of someone you love and care about. With
open arms, He invites you to express your wishes for
your loved one as you humbly accept His will and trust
in His wisdom in all things.

For a member of your family, Christmas this year
may be a time of struggle or hardship. Perhaps there is
illness, financial stress, job loss, or an absent loved one.
Take special time to pray for this person and those con-
cerns you know about. Then say, "I'm keeping you in my
prayers." It's the most meaningful gift you can give, the
most powerful words you can share.

Not to Seek, Lord, but to Share

Dear God, much too often we seek You in prayer
Because we are wallowing in our own self-despair.
We make every word we lamentingly speak
An imperative plea for whatever we seek.
We pray for ourselves and so seldom for others—
We're concerned with our problems and not with our brothers.
We seem to forget, Lord, that the sweet hour of prayer
Is not for self-seeking but to place in Your care
All the lost souls, unloved and unknown,
And to keep praying for them until they're Your own.
For it's never enough to seek God in prayer
With no thought of others who are lost in despair.
So teach us, dear God, that the power of prayer
Is made stronger by placing the world in Your care.

~HSR

In His Care

His name shall be called Wonderful, Counsellor, The mighty God,
The everlasting Father, The Prince of Peace.
Isaiah 9:6 kjv

At this time of year, we happily sing of silent nights and peace on earth; yet we know that in many faraway parts of the world, as well as in nearby neighborhoods and homes, the nights are far from silent and the days are filled with fear and danger. Is peace merely a pious sentiment of a seasonal song?

For God's people, peace is a reality. Peace is not only God's will, but a spiritual gift He gives all who lean on Him and trust in His goodness and mercy. In the birth of Jesus, God sent the Prince of Peace to a warring world, a peace-giver extraordinaire who would bring us into a loving, peaceful, and eternal relationship with our heavenly Father. In Him, we have peace of mind and heart, despite the many tumultuous events around us. We can confidently pray for the peace and safety of all our family members, friends, and brothers and sisters in the faith, particularly those facing threatening situations.

As you hear and sing the tunes of the season, pray for those who have no peace. Place in His loving care embattled countries, cities, neighborhoods, and homes, knowing that in Jesus, the Prince of Peace, there is true and lasting peace for all.

It's a Wonderful World

It's a wonderful world, and it's people like you
Who make it that way by the things that they do.
For a warm, ready smile or a kind, thoughtful deed
Or a hand outstretched in an hour of need
Can change our whole outlook and make the world bright
Where a minute before just nothing seemed right.
It's a wonderful world and it always will be
If we keep our eyes open and focused to see
The wonderful things we are capable of
When we open our hearts to God and His love.

~HSR

A Wonderful Christmas

"See, I am doing a new thing!
Now it springs up; do you not perceive it?"
ISAIAH 43:19 NIV

*P*icture a wonderful Christmas—happy family gathered together, warm fire crackling in the fireplace, Christmas tree heavy with sparkling ornaments and encircled by piles of brightly wrapped gifts. Of course, that wonderful Christmas exists only in our imaginations and on the covers of greeting cards, but its allure sometimes blinds us to the wonders of our real Christmas celebrations.

Real Christmases in every home and in every place are celebrated by real people—people with faults, flaws, and frailties that don't magically disappear at the turn of a calendar page. Real Christmases are made up of real people with annoying personalities, short tempers, and hurt feelings. Real Christmases may bring few gifts, or even no gifts. But in every real Christmas, there are the wonders of Christmas: heart-to-heart conversations, warm memories, and joyous moments.

This year, experience a real Christmas. Keep the eyes and ears of your spirit open to see the real needs and hear the real voices of the people around you. Focus on their good points; look for ways to compliment them; and take time to tell them how much they mean to you. Share with others the love God has for you, and you will find your family celebrating a real and wonderful Christmas.

MAY THE GOOD LORD BLESS AND KEEP YOU ALWAYS

To be in God's keeping is surely a blessing,
For, though life is often dark and distressing,
No day is too dark and no burden too great
That God in His love cannot penetrate.

-HSR

Comfort and Joy

*"Come to Me, all you who labor and are heavy laden,
and I will give you rest."*

MATTHEW 11:28

When your heart is heavy with sadness or sorrow, the last thing you want to do is celebrate the holidays. The carols and bells, the tinsel and evergreens, the shouts of "Merry Christmas!" everywhere you go serve only to remind you of the burden weighing so heavily on your spirit. You want to hide from it all.

Beneath all the hubbub, noise, and trappings of the season, however, lies the Babe of Bethlehem, the One born to lift your sorrows and bring you God's comfort and peace. Because of His life, you have a Friend to go beside you as you walk life's dark and shadowy paths, and you have a Guide to lead you safely across any rough passage. Because He lives, you can place your sorrows in His hands and take your rest in the comfort of His care. At Christmastime and throughout the year, His unconditional love is there for you.

Commit yourself to celebrating Christmas this year, and share the blessings of the season with your family and friends. Allow their voices to lift your spirits, and their caring hearts to ease your sorrow. Lean on God's love for you, and let this Christmas be a time of comfort and joy.

TAKE TIME TO BE KIND

Kindness is a virtue given by the Lord—
It pays dividends in happiness and joy is its reward.
For if you practice kindness in all you say and do,
The Lord will wrap His kindness around your heart and you.

-HSR

TIME FOR KINDNESS

*When the goodness and loving kindness of God
our Savior appeared, he saved us,
not because of works done by us in righteousness,
but according to his own mercy.*

TITUS 3:4–5 ESV

In the weeks leading up to Christmas, time seems to be in especially short supply. There are gifts to be bought, wrapped, and delivered; treats to be mixed, baked, and frosted; ornaments to be placed on the tree. Christmas practices and programs crowd the calendar, and the house is being made ready for company. It's no wonder people worry about having enough time during the holidays!

This busy season is the perfect time to remind yourself to take time for kindness, a gift that costs nothing but a few moments and a warm smile. While shopping, take time to let another person go ahead of you in line, reach an item for a disabled shopper, smile at the checker and exchange a pleasant word. At home, take time to ask about your loved one's day, to listen to his concerns, to help her work out a problem, even when you think you don't have the time. Kindness takes time, but it is the most meaningful and needed gift you can share with others.

As you go about the business of getting ready for Christmas, take time to share the gift of kindness with everyone you meet, and especially with those closest to you in thought and heart.

SHARING WITH FRIENDS

ONLY WITH OUR HEARTS

With our eyes we see the glitter of Christmas,
With our ears we hear its merriment,
With our hands we touch the tinsel-tied trinkets. . . .
But only with our hearts can we feel the miracle of it.

~HSR

The Miracle of Friendship

When they were come into the house, they saw the young child with Mary his mother, and fell down, and worshipped him.

MATTHEW 2:11 KJV

*A*nyone can celebrate the holidays. Anyone can enjoy the carols and songs, the lights and decorations, the traditions, get-togethers, and gifts. But only believers in Jesus can truly appreciate the awesome miracle of this holy season. Only those who come on bended knee to the Babe in the manger can discern the loving heart of God played out in the Christmas story.

In a similar way, anyone can have friends. Anyone can become acquainted with others, enjoy casual conversations with them, and claim them as friends. But only when two people are open to self-forgetfulness, caring and sharing with each other can they appreciate the miracle of friendship. Only when two people see in each other a living soul can they ever discover the loving heart of a dear and beloved friend.

Friendship, like Christmas, is a gift from God to you. Both are designed to lift you up and brighten your life, expanding your dreams and gladdening your heart. In your prayers this season, give thanks for your friends, and show them in some special way how much they mean to you. Throughout the year, remain open to others with whom you may one day come to share the blessing and miracle of friendship.

WHY WRITE THESE CHRISTMAS GREETINGS?

I wonder if you know the real reason
I send you a card every year at this season?
Do you think it's a habit I just can't break
Or something I do just for custom's sake?
I think I should tell you it's something more,
For to me Christmas opens the friendship door....
And I find myself reaching across the year
And clasping the hand of somebody dear.
To me it's a link I wouldn't want broken
That holds us together when words are unspoken.
For often through the year we have to forgo
Exchanging good wishes with those we know,
But Christmas opens the door of the heart
And whether we're close or far apart...
When I write your name I think of you
And pause and reflect and always renew
The bond that exists since we first met
And I found you somebody too nice to forget.

~HSR

Friendship's Door

Two are better than one,
because they have a good return for their work:
If one falls down, his friend can help him up.
Ecclesiastes 4:9–10 NIV

*S*ome people make friends easily. Their keen interest in others, warm smile, and lighthearted ways make them easy to talk to and fun to be around. Other people make friends slowly, often needing to know someone for a long time before they're ready for a deep and comfortable friendship.

However easily or slowly friendship's door swings open for you, you no doubt have found, once you walk through it, that keeping friends and nurturing friendship requires effort. Friendship grows when you go out of your way to spend time with others, and when you actively listen to their cares and concerns. Even when tempted to do otherwise, you forgive their offenses and keep their secrets. You reach out to them when they're down and allow them to comfort you during hard times. As the years go by, true friendship forms, and deep and lasting bonds develop between you and your special friends.

Christmas is the perfect time to connect and reconnect with your friends, especially with those who are part of so many treasured memories. A card, a handwritten note, the sound of your voice—all these things keep the door of friendship open for you and the friends God has so graciously given you.

MAY CHRISTMAS COME AGAIN AND AGAIN

Here's hoping that your Christmas
Is a time that's set apart—
A time that's filled with happiness
And sunshine in your heart. . . .
And may the warmth and love you give
Return to you all year
To brighten days in many ways
And fill your life with cheer!

-HSR

ABUNDANT LOVE

Love one another with brotherly affection.
Outdo one another in showing honor.
ROMANS 12:10 ESV

*H*ave you ever noticed how others pick up on and respond to your moods? For example, when you're feeling happy, other people smile and greet you. They're relaxed and cheerful and friendly. In so many cases, the warmth and love you send out return to you many times over.

When God sent His beloved Son, Jesus, into the world, He presented Himself to you as an unselfish God, willing to give His all for your sake. By His words and through His actions, God opened to you His heart of compassion and love, desiring to receive in return your thanks and praise, your worship, obedience, and affection. He yearns to draw you closer, to strengthen your faith and commitment. He longs to hear your willing and eager *yes* to His work in your life, because God Himself has first said yes to you. Have you responded in kind?

Think of your friends: You do thoughtful things for them, and they respond by doing even more thoughtful things for you. You show you care about them, and they show you in so many ways how much they care about you. With friends, and even more with God, the love you give will come back to you in abundance.

EVERY YEAR WHEN
CHRISTMAS COMES

I have a list of folks I know all written in a book
And every year when Christmas comes, I go and take a look.
And that is when I realize that these names are a part
Not of the book they're written in, but of my very heart.
And while it sounds fantastic for me to make this claim,
I really feel that I'm composed of each remembered name.
So never think my Christmas cards are just a mere routine
Of names upon a Christmas list, forgotten in between,
For I am but the total of the many folks I've met,
And you happen to be one of those I prefer to not forget.
And every year when Christmas comes, I realize anew
The best gift life can offer is meeting folks like you—
And may the spirit of Christmas that forevermore endures
Leave its richest blessings in the hearts of you and yours.

~HSR

Emmanuel

Behold, a virgin shall be with child,
and shall bring forth a son,
and they shall call his name Emmanuel,
which being interpreted is, God with us.
MATTHEW 1:23 KJV

*M*ost likely, your address list has gone through many changes over the years. People move; they marry. Children are born, new friends are added, and elders are released to God's care in death. If you keep an address book the old-fashioned way—pen to paper—the pages tell a story of change!

God's "address," however, remains the same season after season, year after year. You find Him in His book, the Bible, where God tells you about Himself and the kind of God He is—loving, compassionate, caring, and most of all, present. He is as present to you this Christmas as He was present to Christians celebrating Christmas decades ago, right on down to His presence with Mary, Joseph, and the baby Jesus on that first Christmas night. The Bible is the unchangeable book you can open at any time and know you are hearing the voice of God, present for you at all times and in all places.

This year, take time to remember your friends who have recently moved and who may be feeling lonely in their new home or sad to miss their familiar Christmas traditions and celebrations. Encourage them with a note or card telling them about life's unchanging blessing: God's presence in their lives and in His Word at Christmastime and always.

I Think of You and I Pray for You, Too

Often during a busy day
I pause for a minute to silently pray.
I mention the names of those I love
And treasured friends I am fondest of.
For it doesn't matter where we pray
If we honestly mean the words we say,
For God is always listening to hear
The prayers that are made by a heart that's sincere.

~HSR

In Thought, in Prayer

Devote yourselves to prayer,
being watchful and thankful.
Colossians 4:2 niv

Many times throughout the year, and perhaps espe-
cially during the Christmas season, we think of our
friends—how they are doing, how their families are
faring, and where they plan to spend the holidays. And
often with these thoughts comes a short, from-the-heart
prayer asking God to watch over them and bless them
with His joy and peace.

In addition to prayers spoken during worship or
in private devotions, many Christians take pleasure in
offering the gift of prayers for others. These spontane-
ous prayers for friends, loved ones, colleagues, and even
strangers lift up to God our caring thoughts and godly
desires for the encouragement, comfort, and happiness
of others. Also, these prayers are gifts we give ourselves,
for they keep our hearts and minds focused on God, rec-
ognizing Him as creator and giver of all good things.

This Christmas, begin or renew your commitment to
making prayer part of the pattern of your day. When you
think of one of your friends, ask God to bless his day and
guide him in all his ways. When you recall a time spent
with a friend, let your heart speak a few words to God
for strength to meet her challenges and joy to gladden
her soul. Keep friends close in thought—and in prayer.

SOMEBODY CARES

Somebody cares and always will—
The world forgets, but God loves you still.
You cannot go beyond His love
No matter what you're guilty of,
For God forgives until the end—
He is your faithful, loyal Friend. . . .
And though you try to hide your face,
There is no shelter anyplace
That can escape His watchful eye,
For on the earth and in the sky
He's ever-present and always there
To take you in His tender care
And bind the wounds and mend the breaks
When all the world around forsakes.
Somebody cares and loves you still,
And God is the Someone who always will.

~HSR

The Savior Is Born

He was wounded for our transgressions;
he was crushed for our iniquities;
upon him was the chastisement that brought us peace.
Isaiah 53:5 esv

For many of us, the Christmas season brings tension and anxiety. There are troubled family relationships, arguments between friends, offenses remembered, and guilt revived in thought and heart. It's only natural to cover up these uncomfortable facts during this joyful season, yet it's because of the uncomfortable fact of sin that Jesus was born on earth.

The gift of His beloved Son, Jesus, was God's plan from the beginning of time for our forgiveness and salvation. As a perfect and holy God, He could not and would not ignore or cover up the fact that sin has infected our lives and will continue to affect our lives every day we spend this side of heaven. Sin invades our world, our families, our friendships. It touches our bodies when illness strikes, and it soils our spirits when we're burdened with guilt and regret. And sin never takes time off at Christmas!

When the effects of sin threaten your Christmas joy, spend some quiet time reminding yourself that Jesus' birth, life, death, and resurrection have overcome the power of sin and won your forgiveness and salvation. Encourage and lift up your friends who are bowed down by sharing with them the reason for your joy and peace—Christ the Savior is born!

THE WORLD NEEDS FRIENDLY FOLKS LIKE YOU

In this troubled world it's refreshing to find
Someone who still has the time to be kind,
Someone who still has the faith to believe
That the more that you give, the more you receive,
Someone who's ready by thoughts, word, or deed
To reach out a hand in the hour of need.

~HSR

A Difference to One

"I have loved you, my people, with an everlasting love.
With unfailing love I have drawn you to myself."

Jeremiah 31:3 nlt

*M*odern media are good at bringing disasters the world
over right into our homes. In real time, we can watch
the effects of a tsunami thousands of miles away and see
for ourselves the poverty suffered by people crowding
continents far from our own in place and circumstance.
Being exposed to so much, however, can cause us to
feel weak and ineffectual. How much difference, we ask
ourselves, can one person possibly make?

God would have us look at the world not through
the camera's eyes, but through His eyes. Each one of
us makes so much difference to Him that He sent His
beloved Son, Jesus, into our world to rescue us from
eternal disaster and bring us into relationship with Him.
Our need for Him makes such a difference to God that
He promises to hear our prayers, to bless us with all we
need, and to be with us always.

Think about the difference God makes in your life,
and respond by making a difference in the lives of those
around you, especially in the lives of your friends and
loved ones. Perhaps one person cannot change what's
happening across the globe, but one person—you—can
change a friend's world just by being there, by listening,
by serving, by caring.

His Footsteps

When someone does a kindness,
It always seems to me
That's the way God up in heaven
Would like us all to be.
For when we bring some pleasure
To another human heart,
We have followed in His footsteps
And we've had a little part
In serving God who loves us,
For I'm very sure it's true
That in serving those around us,
We serve and please God, too.

-HSR

Following Him

When he saw the multitudes, he was moved with compassion on them,
because they fainted, and were scattered abroad,
as sheep having no shepherd.

Matthew 9:36 KJV

WWJD—What Would Jesus Do?—bracelets became a fad among Christian young people some years ago, but the concept of following in Jesus' footsteps dates back to the time the Lord walked this earth. His early disciples aspired to speak and act the way their Master and Teacher did, and His present-day disciples aspire to the same thing.

Born both God and Man in a humble shelter in Bethlehem, Jesus' earthly life was marked by words and acts of compassion for those He met, particularly humble people who were hurting and had no one to care for them. Jesus offered spiritual guidance and practical help to those who came to Him with sincere hearts, never turning away anyone because of age, status, condition, or circumstance. Our Master's example shows us not only how He responds to us, but how we are to respond to those around us.

Has the Lord put it on your heart this Christmas to bless the life of someone less fortunate than you—say, someone who needs financial assistance, shelter, or a friend who will listen and care? If so, do what Jesus would do, and in doing so, you will be showing your friends what their Lord and Savior did—and still does.

SHARING WITH OTHERS

THE SPIRIT OF GIVING

Each year at Christmas, the spirit of giving
Adds joy to the season and gladness to living.
And knowing this happens when Christmas is here,
Why can't we continue throughout the year
To make our lives happy and abundant with living
By following each day the spirit of giving?

~HSR

Joy for All Seasons

Be steadfast, immovable, always abounding in the work of the Lord,
knowing that your labor is not in vain in the Lord.
1 Corinthians 15:58

When the holidays are over, decorations get packed away and forgotten until next year's season comes around. Unfortunately, along with the tinsel, trim, and baubles of the Christmas tree, our Christmas spirit can get packed away, too—our spirit of sharing and giving that had been so much a part of the season.

God's gift to you in Jesus was no onetime thing, nor was it something He intended for you to think about only once a year. Far from it! Jesus' birth in Bethlehem expresses and shows God's love, for He was willing to come down from heaven and become like you, sharing in your humanity in every way except sin. Jesus' resurrection proves His power over death, along with His ability to raise you on the Last Day and His promise to be present with you now and forever. In Jesus, God shares His love with you every single day of the year.

What special kinds of sharing with others are you doing this Christmas season? Are you serving meals in a shelter for the homeless, donating to a charity for children, helping out a friend in need? Why not continue one or two of your Christmastime activities all year round?

CHRISTMAS IS A SEASON FOR GIVING

Christmas is a season for gifts of every kind—
All the glittery, pretty things that Christmas shoppers find—
Baubles, beads, and bangles of silver and of gold—
Anything and everything that can be bought or sold
Is given at this season to place beneath the tree,
For Christmas is a special time for giving lavishly.
But there's one rare and priceless gift that can't be sold or bought—
It's something poor or rich can give, for it's a loving thought....
And loving thoughts are blessings for which no one can pay,
And only loving hearts can give this priceless gift away.

~HSR

Real Gifts

*"You shall love the Lord your God with all your heart
and with all your soul and with all your strength
and with all your mind, and your neighbor as yourself."*

Luke 10:27 esv

For people who had been living beyond their means on maxed-out credit cards, the recent economic downturn brought not only financial woes but, for many, a whole reordering of their values. As they let go of things they couldn't pay for and adopted a simpler lifestyle, they looked back and wondered why they had risked financial security to buy what has no lasting value.

On that first Christmas, God sent Jesus to earth at the cost of Jesus' suffering and death; but He charges us nothing for His everything. God raised Jesus from the dead, but demands no payment from us for the priceless gift of forgiveness of sins and eternal life with Him in heaven. God's free gifts, given to us simply because of His love for each one of us, are our most valuable possessions, and not one of these blessings has a price tag attached. Why? Because they cannot be bought, only given.

In Jesus, God has shown us an example of what is truly valuable in life, what is the most valuable gift we can offer, and that is love for others. When you share your time, your patience, your compassion—the gift of yourself—with others, you are sharing a real gift, a gift of everlasting value.

EVERY DAY IS A REASON FOR GIVING AND GIVING IS THE KEY TO LIVING

Every day is a reason for giving
And giving is the key to living. . . .
So let us give ourselves away,
Not just today but every day.
And remember, a kind and thoughtful deed
Or a hand outstretched in a time of need
Is the rarest of gifts, for it is a part
Not of the purse but of a loving heart. . . .
And he who gives of himself will find
True joy of heart and peace of mind.

~HSR

The Gift of Giving

Whoever sows sparingly will also reap sparingly,
and whoever sows generously will also reap generously.
2 Corinthians 9:6 niv

Selfless giving means we give to others without expecting anything in return. When we selflessly give of ourselves, however, we will end up receiving far more than we give.

The gift of our time and attention is the kind of gift that touches lives. Our friendly greeting to a stranger may be the nicest thing she has heard all day. Our patience with a speaker we have trouble understanding may provide hope and encouragement to someone struggling with the language. Our kindness and thoughtfulness may touch someone who, in turn, passes on our gift to the next person, and so on, until untold numbers of people have been blessed by one thoughtful act! This kind of selfless giving almost always brings grateful smiles, but even if our kindness is not acknowledged, we will possess the peace of mind that comes with knowing we have done the right thing.

As you go about preparing food, gifts, and cards for your family and friends this Christmas, look for ways you can share simple kindnesses with everyone you meet along the way—cashiers, servers, sales assistants, service representatives, and other customers. You never know whose life you will touch, but you are assured the selfless things you do will richly touch your own many times over.

WISHES FOR THIS CHRISTMAS

May this Christmas season bring you
Many blessings from above,
And may the coming year be filled
With peace and joy and love.

~HSR

TRUE PEACE

With God nothing shall be impossible.
LUKE 1:37 KJV

*F*ew of us would deny that relaxation relieves tension in body and mind, yet most of us rarely take time to relax. We're too worried about having enough time to get everything done, or we feel we simply can't afford the luxury of leisure. During the busy Christmas season when everyone's rushing around, relaxation becomes next to impossible!

God would have you do the impossible when He steps into your life and offers you His peace of mind and heart. He invites you to shed your anxieties and wrap yourself in His presence. He reorders your priorities by the light of His priorities—love of God and love for others—and your tasks and responsibilities fall into their proper place in your life. And what's more, God's peace is free, just as God's Son, Jesus, was born, died, and rose again so you could freely receive the peace of knowing you are a forgiven and beloved child of God.

If the busyness of the season has you thinking relaxation is impossible, respond to your Lord's gracious offer. Relax in the knowledge that true peace rests with the Babe of Bethlehem called the Prince of Peace, Jesus Christ. Let others see the spirit of peace in you.

Everyone Needs Someone

Everybody everywhere, no matter what his station,
Has moments of deep loneliness and quiet desperation,
For this lost and lonely feeling is inherent in mankind,
It is just the spirit speaking as God tries again to find
An opening in the wall man builds against God's touch,
For he feels so sufficient that he doesn't need God much.
So he vainly goes on struggling to find some explanation
For these disturbing, lonely moods of inner isolation,
But the answer keeps eluding him, for in his finite mind,
He does not even recognize that he will never find
The reason for life's emptiness unless he learns to share
The problems and burdens that surround him everywhere;
But when his eyes are opened and he really looks at others,
He begins to see not strangers but people who are brothers.
So open up your hardened hearts and let God enter in;
He only wants to help you a new life to begin,
And every day's a good day to lose yourself in others,
And anytime's a good time to see mankind as brothers,
And this can only happen when you realize it's true
That everyone needs someone and that someone is you.

~HSR

A Matter of Focus

*"Seek the Kingdom of God above all else, and live righteously,
and he will give you everything you need."*
MATTHEW 6:33 NLT

Some people focus on themselves and how to get material things, while others focus on God and how to serve other people. The first group looks for ways to satisfy themselves, and they imagine that the next person, experience, or purchase will fulfill their longing for happiness. The second group looks for ways to please God, and they know that by serving other people without expecting anything in return, they will find joy.

God would have you among the second group, those focused on Him, His will, and the people around you. He knows your longings and desires cannot be and never will be satisfied in anything other than Him, so He constantly works to draw your attention toward His presence in your life. When your focus shifts from yourself to God, you start to recognize what He has done for you in your life, and your heart begins to see the needs of others. God's Spirit at work in you opens the eyes of your soul, and you respond to others with compassion, because you have seen how God responds to you.

Especially during the Christmas season when shelves and shelves of things plead for your attention, keep your focus on God. Through His eyes, focus on Christmas and see the needs of His beloved children.

HEART GIFTS

It's not the things that can be bought
That are life's richest treasures;
It's just the little "heart gifts"
That money cannot measure.
A cheerful smile, a friendly word,
A sympathetic nod,
All priceless little treasures
From the storehouse of our God—
They are the things that can't be bought
With silver or with gold,
For thoughtfulness and kindness
And love are never sold
They are the priceless things in life
For which no one can pay,
And the giver finds rich recompense
In giving them away.

-HSR

The Spirit of Giving

*May the Lord make you increase and
abound in love for one another and for all.*
1 Thessalonians 3:12 esv

"The more you give, the more you get" sounds like a nice thought, but reason says it can't be true. After all, if you give something away, you don't have it anymore, right?

When it comes to love of others, however, the opposite is true. When you let go of those things that keep people apart—distrust, selfishness, fear—and reach out to others in a spirit of kindly acceptance and selfless giving, you never run out of love for others. Instead, your actions draw others toward you and inspire them to treat you with the same qualities of acceptance and giving, and your love grows! You become more confident around others and more apt to share those things that mean the most, namely, genuine affection and true friendship. And love grows!

God's gift to you of Jesus did not diminish God, but extended His great love to you. In mercy and compassion, He sent His Son into the world to show you the depth of His love, a love that remains full and complete for all eternity. It's love designed to grow in you the more you give it away.

Share God's love for you by loving others in thought, word, and action, and see how the more you give, the more you get!

Brighten the Corner
Where You Are

We cannot all be famous or listed in Who's Who,
But every person, great or small, has important work to do....
For seldom do we realize the importance of small deeds
Or to what degree of greatness unnoticed kindness leads....
For it's not the big celebrity in a world of fame and praise,
But it's doing unpretentiously in undistinguished ways
The work that God assigned to us, unimportant as it seems,
That makes our task outstanding and brings
reality to dreams....
So do not sit and idly wish for wider, new dimensions
Where you can put in practice your many good intentions,
But at the spot God placed you, begin at once to do
Little things to brighten up the lives surrounding you....
For if everybody brightened up the spot
on which they're standing
By being more considerate and a little less demanding,
This dark old world would very soon eclipse the evening star
If everybody brightened up the corner where they are.

~HSR

Big Ideas

"The Mighty One has done great things for me—holy is his name."
Luke 1:49 NIV

*P*erhaps you know someone who has big ideas—someone who talks knowingly about solutions to complex problems, but who has no power to put these solutions into practice. Clearly, any big idea, no matter how brilliantly thought out, amounts to nothing but empty words without action.

God's "big idea" in the Garden of Eden was to send a Savior into the world to reunite a holy God with sinful humankind. He planned to send the perfect sacrifice, His only Son, into the world to do for us what we could not do for ourselves. But without the power to carry out His plan, God's big idea would have been nothing more than a good intention. Almighty God possessed the power, and on that first Christmas, He put His power to work. Christ the Savior was born!

The same almighty God who used His power to bring about the means of your salvation has the power to enter your life with His gifts of peace, forgiveness, and renewal. He has the power to bless your life with His big ideas, ideas you can put into practice just by being who you are, where you are. That's a really big idea—one you have the power to act on right now.

SHARING THE RICHNESS
OF CHRISTMAS

Thank You, God, for Everything

Thank You, God, for everything—the big things and the small—
For every good gift comes from God, the Giver of them all,
And all too often we accept without any thanks or praise
The gifts God sends as blessings each day in many ways.
And so at this time we offer up a prayer
To thank You, God, for giving us a lot more than our share.
First, thank You for the little things that often come our way—
The things we take for granted and don't mention when we pray—
The unexpected courtesy, the thoughtful, kindly deed,
A hand reached out to help us in the time of sudden need.
Oh make us more aware, dear God, of little daily graces
That come to us with sweet surprise from never-dreamed-of places.
Then thank You for the miracles we are much too blind to see,
And give us new awareness of our many gifts from Thee.
And help us to remember that the key to life and living
Is to make each prayer a prayer of thanks
and each day a day of thanksgiving.

-HSR

Pick the Best

[Anna] gave thanks to the Lord, and spoke of Him
to all those who looked for redemption in Jerusalem.
LUKE 2:38

If you were offered a free shopping spree in one of your favorite stores, what kinds of things would you look for? If you're like most people, you would immediately set your sights on the most appealing, desirable, and useful merchandise the store has in stock. You would gather for yourself only the best and pass over anything damaged, unappealing, or useless.

When it comes to ourselves and our everyday lives, however, it's easy to fall into the trap of mentally seeing and gathering only our problems and challenges. We focus on what's wrong, what could be better, our most unattractive attributes, all the while neglecting the many appealing, desirable, and useful things God has placed right in front of us for our use, delight, and enjoyment. Isn't that as silly as picking out the worst products when given an opportunity to choose the best a merchant has to offer?

Look around you! Take a few minutes to look at yourself, your life, and all God has given you. Name your everyday blessings, giving thanks and praise to God for each one. As you gather your blessings together in your mind, you will find yourself surrounded with gifts of incalculable value—all yours for the taking!

A Heart Full of Thanksgiving

Everyone needs someone to be thankful for,
And each day of life we are aware of this more,
For the joy of enjoying and the fullness of living
Are found only in hearts that are filled with thanksgiving.

~HSR

AN ATTITUDE OF GRATITUDE

Jesus said, "I praise you, Father, Lord of heaven and earth,
because you have hidden these things from the wise and learned,
and revealed them to little children."
MATTHEW 11:25 NIV

An attitude of gratitude is not something we are born with, nor does having such an attitude exempt us from realistically facing life's trials and problems. Rather, a genuine attitude of gratitude is a gift from God, nurtured in each one of us as we begin to embrace the many ways He reveals His loving-kindness toward us.

A God-given attitude of gratitude goes much deeper than uninformed optimism or a Pollyannaish skip through life. It is much broader in scope and much deeper in knowledge than knee-jerk cynicism. A God-given attitude of gratitude comes with your willingness to see God's blessings and humbly thank Him each day. It gives you the perspective you need to see beyond problems to solutions and balance life's challenges with its many pleasures and delights. A heart grounded in thanksgiving to God for everything is a heart able to shed the light of God's wisdom and truth on whatever life may bring.

Give yourself an attitude check. What are you expecting this Christmas? Are you living this season with heart and mind established in thanksgiving for all He has given you and continues to give you? Pray for His Spirit to work a genuine attitude of gratitude in you!

Beyond Our Asking

More than hearts can imagine or minds comprehend,
God's bountiful gifts are ours without end.
We ask for a cupful when the vast sea is ours,
We pick a small rosebud from a garden of flowers,
We reach for a sunbeam but the sun still abides,
We draw one short breath but there's air on all sides.
Whatever we ask for falls short of God's giving,
For His greatness exceeds every facet of living;
And always God's ready and eager and willing
To pour out His mercy, completely fulfilling
All of man's needs for peace, joy, and rest,
For God gives His children whatever is best.
Just give Him a chance to open His treasures,
And He'll fill your life with unfathomable pleasures—
Pleasures that never grow worn out and faded
And leave us depleted, disillusioned, and jaded—
For God has a storehouse just filled to the brim
With all that man needs, if we'll only ask Him.

-HSR

The Invitation

"You haven't done this before. Ask, using my name, and you will receive, and you will have abundant joy."

John 16:24 NLT

Imagine a loving parent asking a son or daughter, "What do you want for Christmas?" Then imagine that parent's astonishment to hear the child respond not with a squeal of delight, but with a shrug of indifference. "Nothing," the child says and walks away. Why? Because the child believes the parent neither intends nor has the ability to give anything he really wants.

When we fail to respond with excitement and gratitude to God's gracious invitation to ask Him for the desires of our hearts, we are acting just like that indifferent child. Do we think God has no intention of granting our requests? Do we doubt His ability to bless us and our loved ones with all we need to live in accordance with His plan for our lives? Because God sometimes says "no" or "wait" to something we ask for, do we walk away in a spiritual pout, refusing to ask Him for anything again?

God extends an invitation to you to ask Him for all you need and desire, and He promises to hear your requests. You can be sure He has the intention and the power to bless you richly— and you don't need to wait until Christmas morning to enjoy His abundant gifts and thank Him for His generosity!

SHOWERS OF BLESSINGS

Each day there are showers of blessings
Sent from the Father above,
For God is a great, lavish giver,
And there is no end to His love. . . .
And His grace is more than sufficient,
His mercy is boundless and deep,
And His infinite blessings are countless,
And all this we're given to keep
If we but seek God and find Him
And ask for a bounteous measure
Of this wholly immeasurable offering
From God's inexhaustible treasure. . . .
For no matter how big man's dreams are,
God's blessings are infinitely more,
For always God's giving is greater
Than what man is asking for.

-HSR

A Delightful Surprise

If any of you lacks wisdom, let him ask God,
who gives generously to all without reproach,
and it will be given him.
JAMES 1:5 ESV

During the holiday season, many of us have grown to expect crowded shops, harried sales associates, and limited selection the closer we get to Christmas. What a delightful surprise it would be, then, to walk into a spacious store, be greeted by smiling and helpful sales associates, and find just the gift we're looking for! The happy experience would be far beyond what we were expecting!

When you come to your heavenly Father with your requests, be prepared to receive far more than you were expecting, and far more than you were asking for. What God has to give you comes with more excitement and delight than you could imagine. His gifts bring you a full measure of assurance, comfort, and wisdom that would be unknown to you without the generous outpouring of His hand. A humble request in His name opens the floodgates of heaven's richest blessings waiting for you.

Keep the eyes of your heart and spirit open to see and experience more than you expect throughout the Christmas season and beyond. Thank those who delightfully surprise you with their helpfulness and service, and tell others of your happy discovery. Share the happiness of receiving far more than expected from the hand of your heavenly Father.

GIFTS FROM GOD

This brings you a million good wishes and more
For the things you cannot buy in a store—
Like faith to sustain you in times of trial,
A joy-filled heart and a happy smile,
Contentment, inner peace, and love—
All priceless gifts from God above!

-HSR

SPIRITUAL GIFTS

*The fruit of the Spirit is love, joy, peace, patience, kindness,
goodness, faithfulness, gentleness and self-control.*
GALATIANS 5:22–23 NIV

*P*arents see it happen on Christmas morning: Their
young children are so entranced with the ribbons, bows,
and boxes that they pay no attention to the real gifts
inside those wrappings!

Like young children, we often become so dazzled by
the material gifts of this world that we forget all about
the spiritual gifts—the gifts God promises to give us
richly and in abundance. God longs for us to spiritu-
ally notice, pick up, examine, and accept the gifts of His
Spirit so we can start living a fulfilling, productive, and
God-pleasing life. He yearns for us to value those things
that build integrity, character, honesty, truth, and dignity
in our hearts. No longer busying ourselves with a dizzy-
ing array of temporal things, we sense God urging us to
take on eternal things, things strong enough and lasting
enough to carry us through every season of our lives.

Turn away from anything that distracts you from
wholeheartedly accepting the gifts of God's Spirit, the
gifts God desires to give you. Ask Him to grant you the
spiritual maturity you need to fully appreciate the value
of His gifts, and make the commitment to let His gifts
shape your thoughts, words, and actions every day of the
year.

THE ART OF GREATNESS

It's not fortune or fame or worldwide acclaim
That makes for true greatness, you'll find.
It's the wonderful art of teaching the heart
To always be thoughtful and kind!

~HSR

The Way of Greatness

Though he was God, he did not think of equality with God
as something to cling to. Instead, he gave up his divine privileges;
he took the humble position of a slave.

PHILIPPIANS 2:6–7 NLT

*J*esus willingly gave up all the glory and majesty of heaven to come to earth as an infant, born in a nondescript place and reared by two humble working people. During His lifetime, He was scorned by those who measured human worth according to wealth, rank, power, and privilege, but He was revered by those who saw in His miracles and heard in His message the Savior God had promised to send into the world.

In His earthly ministry, Jesus deliberately avoided the trappings of status and privilege and turned away those who wanted to follow Him only because they hoped to live a comfortable life through His miracles. Jesus' true disciples spent long days and nights on the road with Him, endured mockery, and were dismayed by His crucifixion and death before they rejoiced to see their resurrected Lord. Then His disciples, in following the way of humility set before them, persevered in the face of persecution and loss before they saw Him again, face-to-face in heaven.

Worldly fame and admiring glances from others may or may not be part of your discipleship. If not, are you prepared to follow Him anyway? God grant that you are prepared and willing, for this is the way of true greatness!

The Happiness You Already Have

Memories are treasures that time cannot destroy;
They are the happy pathway to yesterday's bright joy.

~HSR

CHERISH THE DAY

Mary kept all these things, and pondered them in her heart.
LUKE 2:19 KJV

*P*hotos of bygone Christmases stir up a lifetime of cherished memories. There was the Christmas when the kids were young; the Christmas when Grandma and Grandpa were here; the Christmas when the first in-law arrived, and then the first grandchild. Open a Christmas album, and you have opened a wealth of memories!

This year, you and your loved ones will make more Christmas memories for you to treasure in the album of your heart. Time will dim the irritations, annoyances, and difficulties so visible to you right now. You will forget about those things that threaten to cloud your Christmas this year, and focus only on what the photo in your hand (or in your heart) shows you—the smiles of those you love and who love you in return.

Use your cherished memories of past Christmases to teach you how to cherish the present Christmas season. Let things worthy of remembrance come forward in your mind and heart, and enjoy these things to their fullest in this present moment. Let the voices and laughter, the stories and giggles delight you today, just as they will when you look back on them. Cherish today, for it holds a wealth of memories for tomorrow.

GIVE LAVISHLY! LIVE ABUNDANTLY!

The more you give, the more you get;
The more you laugh, the less you fret.
The more you do unselfishly,
The more you live abundantly;
The more of everything you share,
The more you'll always have to spare.
The more you love, the more you'll find
That life is good and friends are kind,
For only what we give away
Enriches us from day to day.

~HSR

A Matter of Time

To everything there is a season,
a time for every purpose under heaven.
ECCLESIASTES 3:1

God has given each of us the same number of minutes in an hour and hours in a day. Even the wealthiest among us cannot buy so much as a second, and even the most powerful cannot bring back a minute once it has passed. Time, though possessed by everyone, is our most limited possession!

Yet some people always seem to have time for others. When you're talking with them, you get their full attention. When you need them, you can depend on them to be there for you. These people use their most limited possession—time—to listen and help, to serve and care. Their hours are devoted to others, and their days are filled with activities designed to bring others comfort, happiness, and encouragement. And these people would choose to spend their time no other way, for they find more joy in using time for others than in using it for themselves.

Discover for yourself the joy of sharing your most limited possession—time—with and for others. Maybe you will stop to listen to a friend rather than rush away on your own errands. Maybe you will sit down with a loved one rather than put off a visit for another weekend. Maybe you will be the one who has unlimited time for others.

SHARING THE MEANING
OF CHRISTMAS

THE GIFT OF GOD'S LOVE

For born in a manger at Christmas
as a gift from the Father above,
An Infant whose name was called Jesus
brought mankind the gift of God's love. . . .
And the gifts that we give have no purpose
unless God is part of the giving
And unless we make Christmas a pattern
to be followed in everyday living.

~HSR

CELEBRATE CHRIST

Unto you is born this day in the city of David a Saviour,
which is Christ the Lord.

LUKE 2:11 KJV

A mother prepares a birthday party for her young
son. She bakes his favorite cake, buys treats and favors,
decorates the house with balloons and streamers, and
invites his friends. The birthday boy, eagerly anticipating
his special day, is thrilled when his friends start arriving
for the party. But his excitement dampens and his smile
fades when he realizes a terrible truth—his friends are
enjoying one other, the cake, games, treats, and favors,
but paying no attention whatsoever to him.

The neglected boy's birthday party is like celebrating
Christmas without Christ. The reason we sing joyful car-
ols at Christmas is because Christ was born on earth to
bless all humankind with God's compassion, mercy, and
forgiveness. The reason we come together at Christmas
is to share with one another the good news of a Child
come down from heaven to be our Shepherd, Lord, and
King. That day in December is so special because of
Christ. Without Him, it's just another day.

How can you keep your eyes, mind, and heart on
Christ this Christmas? Look around your home. Would
anyone know who's at the center of your celebration?
Examine your calendar. Does it show you're paying
attention to Christ and His birth?

THE PRICELESS GIFT OF CHRISTMAS

Christmas is a heavenly gift that only God can give—
It's ours just for the asking for as long as we shall live.
It can't be bought or bartered, it can't be won or sold,
It doesn't cost a penny, and it's worth far more than gold.
It isn't bright and gleaming for eager eyes to see—
It can't be wrapped in tinsel or placed beneath a tree. . . .
For the priceless gift of Christmas is meant just for the heart,
And we receive it only when we become a part
Of the kingdom and the glory which is ours to freely take,
For God sent the holy Christ Child at Christmas for our sake.
So take His priceless gift of love—reach out and you receive—
And the only payment that God asks is just that you believe.

~HSR

Free Gift

We love Him because He first loved us.
1 John 4:19

*Y*ou've seen the ads: Free Gift! Trouble is, if you read the fine print, you realize the "gift" isn't free at all. You need to spend a certain amount of money, or attend a seminar, or fill out a questionnaire. In contrast, God's free gift of forgiveness, love, and salvation is yours as you, through the power of His Spirit at work in you, turn to Him with a repentant heart.

Jesus' birth into the world happened not because you or anyone else spent a required amount of money or met certain conditions first, but because He knows your needs and He cares about you. He knows, too, that neither you nor anyone else could do anything to earn or qualify for a personal relationship with Him, so He simply came and offered Himself. Free.

Are you burdened by the suspicion that you must somehow pay for Jesus to come into your heart or earn your way to forgiveness? It's a natural feeling, but a feeling contrary to the reason Jesus was born into the world. Jesus came to offer the free gift of God's love to all, to everyone—to you. Will you accept His priceless gift without trying to earn it first? Because "free" is the only way He's offering it!

In Christ, Who was Born at Christmas, All Men May Live Again

Let us all remember when our faith is running low,
Christ is more than just a figure wrapped in an ethereal glow. . . .
For He came and dwelled among us and He knows our every need,
And He loves and understands us and forgives each sinful deed.
He was crucified and buried and rose again in glory,
And His promise of salvation makes the wondrous Christmas story
An abiding reassurance that the little Christ Child's birth
Was the beautiful beginning of God's plan for peace on earth.

~HSR

Prince of Peace

"Glory to God in the highest,
and on earth peace to men on whom his favor rests."
Luke 2:14 NIV

In many ways, faith in Christ is like the waters of an expansive, scenic lake. When the sky is clear and the sun is shining, the crystal waters sparkle and birds soar and swoop over the rippling surface. When times are good and everything's going our way, our faith is strong and vibrant! It sparkles! But just as a sudden storm can turn a placid lake into a roiling cauldron, life's storms can whip up doubts about God and His love for us. Our faith ebbs as we mull over nagging questions and spiritual mysteries, and fierce waves of distrust wash over our soul.

Jesus' birth, death, and resurrection took place so we can possess peace amid life's storms. In our times of doubt, He reassures us of His presence in our lives; and in our times of distrust, He encourages us to lean on Him and experience His power and strength. When the troubles of life threaten our spiritual well-being, He comes to still the storms and bring true and lasting peace.

Today, bring to your Lord and God all the storms of your life—the storms within you and the storms around you. Experience for yourself why He is called the Prince of Peace.

A Christmas Prayer

Oh Father up in heaven, we have wandered far away
From the little holy Christ Child that was born on Christmas Day,
And the peace on earth you promised we have been unmindful of,
Not believing we could find it in a simple thing called love.
We've forgotten why You sent us Jesus Christ, Your only Son,
And in arrogance and ignorance it's our will, not Thine, be done.
Oh, forgive us, heavenly Father; teach us how to be more kind
So that we may judge all people with our hearts and not our minds....
Oh, forgive us, heavenly Father, and help us to find the way
To understand each other and live Christmas every day.

~HSR

THE REAL CHRISTMAS

Everyone who believes that Jesus
is the Christ has been born of God.
1 John 5:1 ESV

*T*he real Christmas takes place not in a home or a church, or at a certain time or in a particular location. Rather, the real Christmas happens in the human heart—a heart willing to humbly receive the gift of God's love in Jesus. In other words, the real Christmas can take place anywhere and at any time!

While the Christmas season is here, it's easy to remember to give to charity, share with others, visit the lonely, and wish our loved ones, friends, associates, and even strangers all the blessings of the season. But as we leave behind the festivities and get down to the business of the new year, we tend to leave behind our Christmas spirit as well. We forget about giving to those less fortunate than ourselves, about sharing with and caring for others, about extending a friendly greeting to those we meet. We forget all about the real Christmas, the one that happens every day.

During the Christmas season, bring Christmas into your heart by meditating on the reason why Christ was born into the world and planning your response to His gift of love. Then make yourself a reminder note so you will remember, when the season is over, to live the real meaning each day of the new year.

BEHOLD, I BRING YOU GOOD TIDINGS OF GREAT JOY

Glad tidings herald the Christ child's birth—
Joy to the world and peace on earth,
Glory to God... Let all men rejoice
And hearken once more to the angel's voice.
It matters not who or what you are—
All men can behold the Christmas star,
For the star that shone is shining still
In the hearts of men of peace and goodwill.
It offers the answer to every man's need,
Regardless of color or race or creed....
So joining together in brotherly love,
Let us worship again our Father above,
And forgetting our own little selfish desires,
May we seek what the star of Christmas inspires.

-HSR

The Christmas Star

"We have seen His star in the East and have come to worship Him."
MATTHEW 2:2

The things that keep us apart are many. Old offenses and differing opinions strain family relationships. Matters of race, religion, and politics put groups of people on opposing sides. Suspicion and distrust between nations lead to failed diplomatic efforts, standoffs, and war.

The message of Christmas, however, continues to echo through the ages and throughout the world, reminding us of God's equal and abundant love for all of us—the in-law with the grating personality, the neighbor of another race, the citizen of a belligerent regime. Jesus was born for all! The star of Bethlehem shone in the sky to bring all of us to the humble place of His birth, to gather all of us on bended knee at the side of His manger bed. God, in sending a Savior into the world, opened salvation to all the world.

God's love and compassion for you invite you to respond by extending love and compassion to others. Celebrate the unity you have with all believers in Christ, no matter who they are or where they live. Welcome everyone who asks about the Babe born in a stable on that first Christmas long ago. Share with them the good news of the love God shares abundantly with you.

FOREVER THANKS

Give thanks for the blessings that daily are ours—
The warmth of the sun, the fragrance of flowers.
With thanks for all the thoughtful,
caring things you always do
And a loving wish for happiness today
and all year through!

-HSR

A Word of Thanks

Give thanks to the God of heaven. His faithful love endures forever.
PSALM 136:26 NLT

After the gifts have been opened, the thank-you notes come out. Or do they? "Not often enough," declares the aunt who has yet to hear a word of thanks for the presents she sent her nieces and nephews last year.

Christmas is a good time to remind ourselves how important it is to be thankful in word and action. We say and show our gratitude to God for the gift of His Son, Jesus, when we gladly and faithfully gather in His house to worship Him, singing His praises and giving Him our thanks for all He has done and continues to do for us. We say and show our gratitude for the kindness and goodness of others when we take the time to mention how much their thoughtfulness means to us, to write those thank-you notes, and to keep in touch throughout the year.

If it has been a long time since you have expressed your thanks to God for His gift of love in Jesus, tell Him now. If there is someone in your life who needs to hear your words of gratitude, speak those words today. Miss no opportunity to give thanks in word and action!

A Christmas Blessing

May Jesus, our Savior, who was born on Christmas Day,
Bless you at this season in a very special way.
May the beauty and the promise of that silent, holy night
Fill your heart with peace and happiness
and make your new year bright.

~HSR

WHEN WISHES COME TRUE

All flesh shall see the salvation of God.
LUKE 3:6 KJV

*F*or many, especially children, Christmas is a time when they hope their wishes come true. They wish for a bicycle, a computer game, a cell phone. But without someone to actually buy those gifts for them, their wish remains just that—a wish.

When we wish others a Merry Christmas and a Happy New Year, those wishes remain empty phrases and meaningless sentiments unless we take action to help someone's Christmas become a joyous occasion and lift someone's burden to make happiness possible during the new year. Our repeated holiday wishes for others come true not by buying things, but by doing things—things like putting the needs and desires of others before our own; offering practical and timely assistance to those who struggle with life's challenges; being there for those in need of friendship, compassion, and encouragement.

What can you do this Christmas to make the holidays more cheerful for someone else? What can you do throughout the new year to bring happiness to others? Make a list of specific things you can do this season to make Merry Christmas more than a wish, and particular actions you can take to turn Happy New Year into a daily reality for yourself and others.

A Prayer for Christmas

God, give us eyes this Christmas to see the Christmas star,
And give us ears to hear the song of angels from afar. . . .
And with our eyes and ears attuned for a message from above,
Let Christmas angels speak to us of hope and faith and love—
Hope to light our pathway when the way ahead is dark,
Hope to sing through stormy days with the sweetness of a lark,
Faith to trust in things unseen and know beyond all seeing
That it is in our Father's love we live and have our being,
And love to break down barriers of color, race, and creed,
Love to see and understand and help all those in need.

~HSR